Quranic Calligraphy

All rights reserved. 2025
No part of this publication may be reproduced, stored in a retrieval system, or transmitted in any form or by any means, whether electronic, mechanical, photocopying, recording, or by any other process, without prior authorization.

Typographic Foundations

LET'S KEEP IT SIMPLE—MODERN CALLIGRAPHY ISN'T ABOUT RIGID RULES OR ANCIENT TRADITIONS. INSTEAD, IT'S ALL ABOUT FREEDOM, CREATIVITY, AND ADDING YOUR PERSONAL FLAIR TO EVERY STROKE. BUT HERE'S THE SECRET: GOOD POSTURE, A PROPER GRIP, AND THE RIGHT PAPER ARE THE FOUNDATIONS THAT HELP YOUR CREATIVITY FLOW EFFORTLESSLY. MASTERING THESE BASICS WILL SET YOU UP TO LET YOUR STYLE SHINE AND YOUR PEN DANCE ACROSS THE PAGE

Body

THINK POSTURE DOESN'T MATTER? THINK AGAIN! IN MODERN CALLIGRAPHY, FLUID MOTION AND EASE ARE EVERYTHING. SIT COMFORTABLY—MAYBE AT A DESK WHERE YOUR FEET REST FLAT ON THE GROUND AND YOUR ARM HAS THE SPACE TO GLIDE FREELY. THE MAGIC HAPPENS WHEN YOUR WHOLE ARM GETS INVOLVED, NOT JUST YOUR FINGERS. IMAGINE YOU'RE CHOREOGRAPHING A DANCE WITH EVERY STROKE—GRACEFUL, INTENTIONAL, AND FULL OF MOVEMENT

Pen

YOUR PEN IS YOUR CREATIVE WAND, AND IN MODERN CALLIGRAPHY, THERE'S NO "ONE SIZE FITS ALL." WHETHER IT'S A BRUSH PEN, FINELINER, OR MARKER, THE BEST TOOL IS THE ONE YOU FEEL MOST CONNECTED TO. HOLD IT AT AN ANGLE WITH A GENTLE YET SECURE GRIP. DON'T STRESS OVER PERFECTION—YOUR FIRST LINES ARE MEANT TO WOBBLE. THAT'S WHERE THE FUN BEGINS! MODERN CALLIGRAPHY IS ALL ABOUT EXPERIMENTING, LEARNING, AND LETTING YOUR STYLE EVOLVE NATURALLY.

Tools for Quranic Calligraphy

IF YOU'RE FEELING ADVENTUROUS, YOU CAN EASILY LOSE YOURSELF IN THE ENDLESS WORLD OF CRAFT SUPPLIES—AND YES, IT'S TEMPTING TO SPEND A SMALL FORTUNE! IF THAT'S YOUR VIBE, GO FOR IT! BUT HERE, WE'LL KEEP THINGS SIMPLE. ALL YOU REALLY NEED IS A TRUSTY FUDENOSUKE PEN AND A BRUSH PEN TO GET STARTED. STILL, IF YOU'RE CURIOUS, HERE'S A BREAKDOWN OF SOME POPULAR TOOLS YOU MIGHT WANT TO TRY:

★ PENCILS

THE ULTIMATE STARTING POINT—SIMPLE, HUMBLE, AND ALWAYS RELIABLE. PERFECT FOR SKETCHING OUT YOUR DESIGNS BEFORE DIVING IN.

★ PENS

FEELING UNSURE? START WITH A PEN! FINELINERS ARE A SAFE BET, BUT DON'T SHY AWAY FROM MARKERS OR GEL PENS FOR SMOOTH, BOLD MONOLINE STROKES.

★ BRUSH PENS

THINK OF THESE AS THE MODERN VERSION OF THE ELEGANT QUILL PENS OF OLD—BUT WAY MORE FUN TO USE. WARNING: THEY'RE ADDICTIVE. START WITH A SMALLER, FIRMER BRUSH PEN TO GAIN BETTER CONTROL WHILE PRACTICING YOUR ARM MOVEMENTS.

★ WATERCOLORS

READY TO TAKE IT UP A NOTCH? WATERCOLORS ADD A SPLASH OF ARTISTRY TO YOUR CALLIGRAPHY. SWAP OUT BRUSHES FOR DIFFERENT EFFECTS AND LET YOUR CREATIVITY FLOW. PLAY AROUND AND EMBRACE THE BEAUTY OF EXPERIMENTATION!

Tools for Quranic Calligraphy

★ CHALK

CHALK MARKERS ARE A GAME-CHANGER. WITH A LITTLE PRACTICE, YOU'LL BE CREATING STUNNING CHALKBOARD DESIGNS IN NO TIME. FROM CAFE MENUS TO SIDEWALK ART, CHALK CALLIGRAPHY HAS A CHARM THAT'S HARD TO RESIST.

★ PAPER

WHILE THIS BOOK GIVES YOU PLENTY OF SPACE TO PRACTICE, EXPERIMENTING WITH DIFFERENT PAPERS CAN MAKE A HUGE DIFFERENCE. TRY HEAVIER MATERIALS LIKE CARDSTOCK FOR SMOOTHER STROKES AND BETTER INK ABSORPTION. AVOID THIN PAPER, LIKE STANDARD PRINTER PAPER—IT CAN BE FRUSTRATING TO WORK WITH AND MIGHT RUIN YOUR FLOW.

★ FUDENOSUKE PEN

THIS FINE-LINER MARKER IS A GO-TO TOOL FOR MONOLINE WRITING. SIMPLE, PRECISE, AND WIDELY AVAILABLE IN CRAFT STORES, IT'S PERFECT FOR MASTERING CLEAN, UNIFORM LINES.

★ BRUSHES

BRUSH PENS ARE YOUR VERSATILE ALLIES IN MODERN CALLIGRAPHY. USE THEM FOR BOLD BRUSH CALLIGRAPHY OR TO ADD INTRICATE FLORAL ACCENTS. THEY'RE IDEAL FOR EXPLORING BOTH LETTERING AND DECORATIVE ELEMENTS IN YOUR DESIGNS.

Terminology

BEFORE YOU CAN START CREATING BEAUTIFUL LETTERS, IT'S ESSENTIAL TO GET FAMILIAR WITH SOME KEY TERMS. THINK OF IT AS LEARNING THE ALPHABET BEFORE WRITING WORDS— SO DON'T SKIP THIS PART! UNDERSTANDING THE BASICS WILL MAKE YOUR CALLIGRAPHY JOURNEY MUCH SMOOTHER.

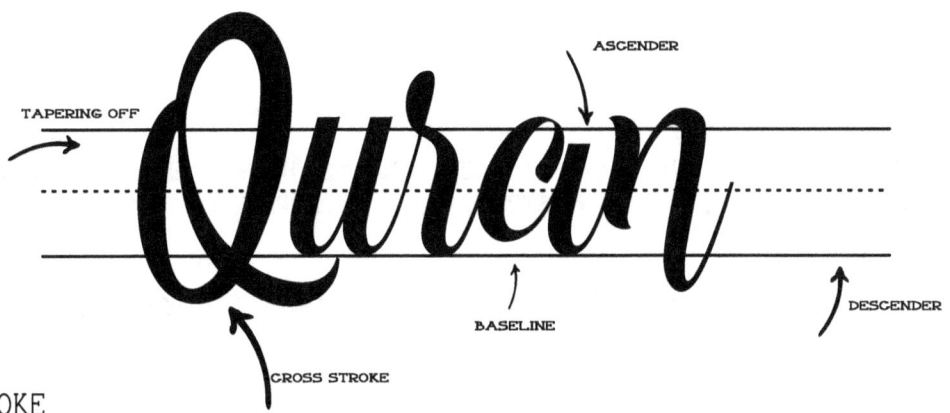

★ DESCENDING STROKE

ANY DOWNWARD MOVEMENT OF YOUR WRITING TOOL. THESE STROKES ARE TYPICALLY THICKER, ADDING WEIGHT AND DEPTH TO YOUR LETTERS.

★ ASCENDING STROKE

ANY UPWARD MOVEMENT OF YOUR WRITING TOOL. THESE STROKES ARE THINNER, CREATING A LIGHT AND GRACEFUL CONTRAST.

★ ASCENDER

THE PART OF A LETTER THAT STRETCHES ABOVE THE MEDIAN LINE—FOR EXAMPLE, THE UPPER PORTION OF A "T" OR "H."

★ DESCENDER

THE PART OF A LETTER THAT DROPS BELOW THE BASELINE, LIKE THE TAIL OF A "G" OR "Y."

★ FLOW

DECORATIVE STROKES OR ARROWS ADDED TO YOUR LETTERS TO GIVE THEM EXTRA FLAIR AND PERSONALITY.

★ CROSSBAR

THE HORIZONTAL STROKE IN LETTERS SUCH AS "T," "F," OR UPPERCASE "H."

★ LETTERFORM

THE OVERALL SHAPE AND STRUCTURE OF A LETTER—ITS UNIQUE IDENTITY AND STYLE.

Tips for Quranic Calligraphy

ONE
SLOW AND STEADY WINS THE RACE! TREAT EACH LETTER AS A TINY WORK OF ART, DRAWING IT WITH CARE INSTEAD OF RUSHING THROUGH LIKE ORDINARY HANDWRITING.

TWO
BEGIN WITH A PENCIL—IT'S YOUR BEST FRIEND. SKETCH, ERASE, AND REFINE YOUR LETTERS UNTIL THEY LOOK JUST RIGHT. MISTAKES ARE PART OF THE PROCESS!

THREE
LIFT YOUR PEN AFTER EACH STROKE. UNLIKE CURSIVE WRITING, WHERE THE PEN GLIDES CONTINUOUSLY ACROSS THE PAGE, MODERN CALLIGRAPHY IS BUILT STROKE BY STROKE, GIVING YOU MORE CONTROL AND PRECISION.

FOUR
REMEMBER THE GOLDEN RULE: DOWNWARD STROKES ARE ALWAYS THICKER. THIS CREATES THE SIGNATURE CONTRAST THAT MAKES CALLIGRAPHY SO BEAUTIFUL.

FIVE
ON THE FLIP SIDE, UPWARD STROKES SHOULD ALWAYS BE LIGHT AND THIN. LET YOUR HAND GLIDE SOFTLY TO ACHIEVE THAT GRACEFUL TOUCH.

SIX
PRACTICE, PRACTICE, PRACTICE! START BY MASTERING INDIVIDUAL LETTERFORMS, THEN WORK ON CONNECTING LETTERS TO FORM WORDS. ONCE YOU FEEL CONFIDENT, EXPLORE FULL COMPOSITIONS AND ADD CREATIVE FLOURISHES TO MAKE YOUR WORK UNIQUE.

IN THE NEXT SECTION, WE'LL DIVE INTO THE BASICS—DRAWING THE FOUNDATIONAL STROKES AND CREATING STUNNING LETTERFORMS!

GRAB YOUR PENCILS, PENS, AND BRUSHES—IT'S TIME TO BRING YOUR CREATIVITY TO LIFE. YOUR LETTERING JOURNEY STARTS NOW!

Basic strokes
INTRODUCTION

ALSO CALLED "FAUX CALLIGRAPHY," THESE STROKES ARE A PERFECT STARTING POINT. WHILE I LOVE THE IDEA OF THOSE THICK, BOLD STROKES, IN PRACTICE, I'M ALL ABOUT MONOLINE. IT'S QUICKER, SIMPLER (IN MY OPINION), AND BRINGS OUT MY INNER PINTEREST CRAFT QUEEN!

THE TECHNIQUE MIRRORS BRUSH LETTERING MOVEMENTS, BUT INSTEAD OF VARYING PRESSURE, YOU KEEP IT CONSISTENT THROUGHOUT—NO THICK DOWNWARD STROKES HERE. GRAB A PENCIL OR A FINE-TIP PEN (THE SMALLER, THE BETTER), AND GET READY TO CREATE WITH EASE!

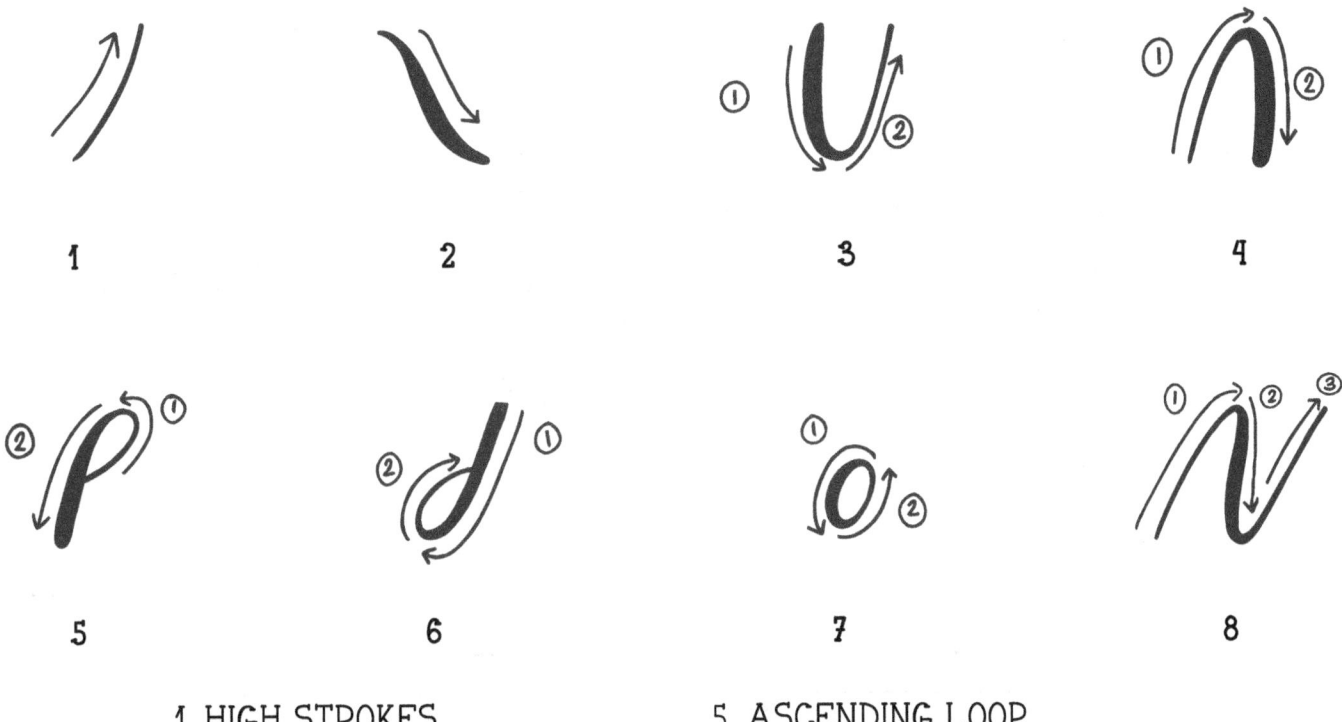

1. HIGH STROKES
2. LOW STROKES
3. BACKSTROKE
4. REVERSE STROKE
5. ASCENDING LOOP
6. DESCENDING LOOP
7. OVAL
8. COMPOUND CURVE

High Strokes

- BEGIN FROM THE BOTTOM AND MOVE UPWARD IN A SMOOTH MOTION.
- KEEP THE STROKE THIN AND CONSISTENT FOR A CLEAN LOOK.
- APPLY LIGHT PRESSURE TO MAINTAIN THE DELICATE, GRACEFUL FLOW.

Downward Strokes

- UNLIKE UPWARD STROKES, BEGIN AT THE TOP AND MOVE DOWNWARD, APPLYING MORE PRESSURE FOR A THICKER LINE.
- START WITH MEDIUM PRESSURE AT THE TOP, GRADUALLY INCREASING AS YOU MOVE DOWN TO CREATE A BOLD, SMOOTH STROKE.
- EASE OFF THE PRESSURE AT THE END FOR A SOFT, TAPERED FINISH.

Upturn

Turnaround

- BEGIN WITH AN UPWARD STROKE, APPLYING LIGHT, CONSISTENT PRESSURE TO CREATE A THIN LINE.

- SMOOTHLY TRANSITION INTO A DOWNWARD STROKE BY INCREASING PRESSURE AS YOU MOVE DOWNWARD.

- THE KEY IS A SEAMLESS FLOW—PRACTICE BLENDING THE THIN UPWARD LINE INTO THE THICKER DOWNWARD STROKE FOR A POLISHED LOOK.

Ascending Loop

Descending Loop

Oval

Compression of Turns

11

Basic Calligraphy

UPPERCASE ALPHABET

A A A A A A

B B B B B B B

C C C C C C C

D D D D D D D

E E E E E E E

F F F F F F F

G G G G G G G

Practice Sheet

Basic Calligraphy

UPPERCASE ALPHABET

H

I

J

K

L

M

N

Practice Sheet

Basic Calligraphy
UPPERCASE ALPHABET

O O O O O O O O O

P P P P P P P P P

Q Q Q Q Q Q Q Q Q

R R R R R R R R R

S S S S S S S S S

T T T T T T T T T

U U U U U U U U U

Practice Sheet

Basic Calligraphy

UPPERCASE ALPHABET

V

W

X

Y

Z

Practice Sheet

Basic Calligraphy
SMALL LETTERS OF THE ALPHABET

a a a a a a a a a

b b b b b b b b b

c c c c c c c c c

d d d d d d d d d

e e e e e e e e e

f f f f f f f f f

g g g g g g g g g

Practice Sheet

Basic Calligraphy

SMALL LETTERS OF THE ALPHABET

h

i

j

k

l

m

n

Practice Sheet

Basic Calligraphy

SMALL LETTERS OF THE ALPHABET

o o o o o o o o o o o

p p p p p p p p p p p

q q q q q q q q q q q

r r r r r r r r r r r

s s s s s s s s s s s

t t t t t t t t t t t

u u u u u u u u u u u

Practice Sheet

Basic Calligraphy

SMALL LETTERS OF THE ALPHABET

v v v v v v v v

w w w w w w w w

x x x x x x x x

y y y y y y y y

z z z z z z z z

Practice Sheet

Basic Calligraphy
NUMERIC DIGITS

0 0 0 0 0 0 0 0

1 1 1 1 1 1 1 1

2 2 2 2 2 2 2 2

3 3 3 3 3 3 3 3

4 4 4 4 4 4 4 4

5 5 5 5 5 5 5 5

6 6 6 6 6 6 6 6

Practice Sheet

My Success IS ONLY By ALLAH

Basic Calligraphy
NUMERIC DIGITS

7 7 7 7 7 7 7 7 7

8 8 8 8 8 8 8 8 8

9 9 9 9 9 9 9 9 9

Practice Sheet

Basic Calligraphy

CORE BELIEFS AND PILLARS OF ISLAM

Allah

Faith

Islam

Tawheed

Ihsan

Sunnah

Quran

Practice Sheet

Basic Calligraphy

CORE BELIEFS AND PILLARS OF ISLAM

Hadith

Ummah

Sharia

Shahada

Salat

Saum

Hajj

Practice Sheet

Basic Calligraphy

ESSENTIAL ISLAMIC VALUES

Patience

Charity

Justice

Mercy

Forgiveness

Peace

Blessings

Practice Sheet

Basic Calligraphy

RAMADAN AND ACTS OF WORSHIP

Ramadan

Eid

Salah

Zakat

Barakah

Jannah

Taqwa

Practice Sheet

Basic Calligraphy

PROPHETS, PLACES, AND SACRED SYMBOLS

Muhammad

Ibrahim

Musa

Isa

Maryam

Kaaba

Mecca

Practice Sheet

Basic Calligraphy

ESSENTIAL ISLAMIC PHRASES FOR DAILY LIFE

Bismillah

Alhamdulillah

Subhan Allah

Allahu Akbar

Astaghfirullah

Insha Allah

Mash Allah

Practice Sheet

WHEN LIFE
Gets Harder
CHALLENGE
Yourself
TO BE
Stronger

Basic Calligraphy

RAMADAN & EID BLESSINGS FOR REFLECTION

Ramadan Mubarak

Eid Mubarak

May your fasts be accepted

Seek peace through patience

May Allah bless your family

Worship with sincerity

The best charity is given in secret

Practice Sheet

Basic Calligraphy
ISLAMIC PRAYERS & BLESSINGS FOR INNER PEACE

Allah guide you

Heart filled with Noor

Trust Allah's plan

Increase your blessings

Pray, then let go

Allah knows best

May Allah grant peace

Practice Sheet

WHEN LIFE Gets HARDER Challenge YOURSELF TO Be Stronger

Basic Calligraphy
WORDS OF STRENGTH & PATIENCE

Have patience

Stay strong in faith

Allah is with you

Hardship brings ease

Seek strength in prayer

Faith over fear

Trust His wisdom

Practice Sheet

Basic Calligraphy

GRATITUDE & BLESSINGS

Be grateful always

Blessings multiply

Say Alhamdulillah

Allah provides

Grateful hearts shine

Give with sincerity

Thankfulness brings peace

Practice Sheet

Basic Calligraphy
GUIDANCE & WISDOM

Walk the right path

Seek divine wisdom

Light in your heart

Knowledge is a gift

Follow the truth

Guided by faith

Wisdom through patience

Practice Sheet

BE THE
New
CHANGE FOR
Yourself In
THE DAYS
Of Ramadan

Basic Calligraphy
PEACE & SPIRITUAL REFLECTION

Find peace in faith

Calm your heart

Faith brings serenity

Noor in your soul

Let go, trust Allah

Dua heals hearts

Peace be upon you

Practice Sheet

Basic Calligraphy
INSPIRING QUOTES TO TRACE

Practice Sheet

Basic Calligraphy
INSPIRING QUOTES TO TRACE

58

Practice Sheet

YOU CAN STILL MAKE OR BREAK A HABIT

Basic Calligraphy
INSPIRING QUOTES TO TRACE

"I would like to express my gratitude for purchasing this book. I would be immensely thankful if you could take a moment to share your feedback. This greatly helps the growth of our small business and allows us to reach more people.."

www.ingramcontent.com/pod-product-compliance
Lightning Source LLC
LaVergne TN
LVHW060336080526
838202LV00053B/4488